GOODNIGHT SAN ANTONIO

Viva San Antonio! ☆

Written by *Jennifer Drez*

Jennifer Gaines Drez

Illustrated by

Lisa Carrington Voight

Published by JGD Publishing, LLC
Fort Worth, Texas

Goodnight San Antonio
Library of Congress Control Number: 2012922329
ISBN-13: 978-0-9886023-0-4 / ISBN-10: 0-9886-0230-4
First Edition- 2013
Illustrations by Lisa Carrington Voight using acrylic paint on canvas
Graphic design by Cynthia Wahl
Printed in Canada

To order additional copies of this book, please visit goodnightsanantonio.com

Goodnight San Antonio is dedicated to our families
and to the wonderful people of San Antonio.
Without your help, this book would not have been possible.

The sun is setting on the city of culture and heritage.

It's time to say goodnight to San Antonio
and all that we cherish.

Goodnight Casa Rio,
tourists and laughter.

Goodnight mariachis and flamencos at the Arneson Theater.

Goodnight to the Spanish Governor's Palace and to the San Fernando Cathedral.

Goodnight to the Menger
and the ghosts
who linger.

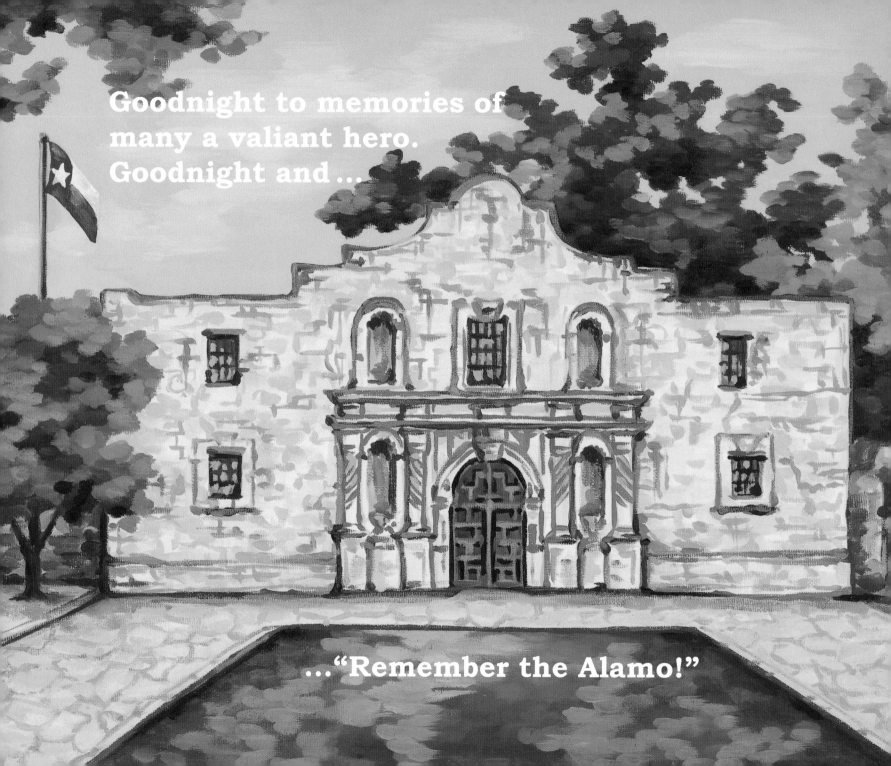

Goodnight to memories of
many a valiant hero.
Goodnight and ...

..."Remember the Alamo!"

Goodnight to the missions and the history they convey.

Goodnight Concepción and San Juan, Espada and San José.

Goodnight Magik Theatre and HemisFair Park.
Goodnight Tower of the Americas
and fireworks after dark.

Goodnight to men and women in uniform, who wear the flag with pride.

Thank you for defending our freedom worldwide.

Goodnight Hall of Horns,
cowboy boots and
Paris Hatters.

Goodnight to the rodeo, cowboys and entertainers.

Buenas noches El Mercado y Mi Tierra.

Buenas noches Teatro Guadalupe y Veladora.

Goodnight to
concerts and to
the Symphony.

Goodnight to the
Majestic and creativity.

Goodnight
to chili and
spices we
hold dear.

Goodnight
to Schilo's,
Reubens and
root beer.

Goodnight to the Alamodome,
concerts and football.

Goodnight to the Spurs
and players so tall.

Goodnight
Museum Reach
and foodies at
Pearl Brewery.

Goodnight SAMA and beautiful scenery.

Goodnight to the Tea Garden,
the waterfall and the koi.

Goodnight to the Eagle
and Kiddie Park
we enjoy.

Goodnight to all of the animals at the zoo.

Goodnight to the treehouse at the Witte, too.

Goodnight conservatories and garden displays.

Goodnight to sculpture and art at the McNay.

Goodnight to books on history and lessons of diversity.

Goodnight to the library.

Goodnight historic
homes in the
King William District.

Goodnight to the
Guenther House,
waffles and biscuits.

Goodnight to Fiesta®, parties and parades.

Goodnight to the royalty as they promenade.

Goodnight to rollercoasters, shrieks and squeals.
Goodnight to sealife, orcas and seals.

Goodnight to the caverns, stalagmites and stalactites.

Goodnight to the Hill Country, bluebonnets and starry nights.

Goodnight San Antonio, the city of fiestas!
Goodnight San Antonio, the soul of Texas!

Acknowledgements

San Antonio is a dynamic, culturally rich city, which this book only begins to explore. It is our hope that *Goodnight San Antonio* helps to foster an even deeper sense of pride in children and adults about a city filled with wonderful history and culture.

We thank several San Antonio enthusiasts for their support and help in making this book become a reality. Without them it would not have been possible. We also appreciate the support of the establishments mentioned in *Goodnight San Antonio* and hope they live on in the hearts and minds of this generation and many more to come.

--- ★ ---

San Antonio

San Antonio began as a Native American village. The area was called Yanaguana due to the winding of the San Antonio River. On June 13, 1691, Saint Anthony of Padua's feast day, Spanish explorers discovered the area and named it San Antonio de Bejar in the Saint's honor.

San Antonio was the largest Spanish Settlement in Texas and is famous for its five Spanish missions. Early settlers to the area came from many countries, creating a rich history with strong cultural influences from Mexico, Spain, France, Germany and the American South. The area was the site of revolutions and wars leading up to when Texas joined the United States in 1845. This strong military presence continues today, as San Antonio is home to several important military bases.

Due to its rich heritage, San Antonio was chosen to host the 1968 World's Fair and the theme was "Confluence of Cultures in the Americas." The varied cultural influences have created a beautiful and vibrant city filled with celebrations and fiestas.

San Antonio River Walk (Paseo del Rio)

The River Walk is a pedestrian walkway below street level that winds alongside the San Antonio River. It is lined with restaurants, shops, hotels and bars. The walkways wind and loop connecting major attractions from the Alamo all the way to Pearl Brewery.

Casa Rio

Casa Rio, a 4th generation family-owned business founded in 1946 by Alfred Beyer, was the first San Antonio business to open on the scenic San Antonio River. The restaurant is a popular destination on the River Walk and is known for its traditional Tex-Mex fare. The family also started the first river tour and dinner boats.

Arneson River Theater

This open-air venue erected in 1939 is named for Edwin Arneson, who was instrumental in securing funding for the Paseo del Rio (the River Walk). The venue is part of La Villita. The stage is on the north side of the river and the audience sits on the grass-covered steps on the south side.

La Villita Historic Arts Village

Early Spanish soldiers stationed at Mission San Antonio de Valero (the Alamo) settled in this area, making it San Antonio's first neighborhood. In the 19th century, German-French immigrants moved into La Villita, creating a strong city center. The neighborhood was restored in the late 1930s, becoming the first arts district in San Antonio.

San Fernando Cathedral

Founded in 1731 by settlers from the Canary Islands, San Fernando Cathedral is among the oldest Catholic parish churches in the Southwest and is the oldest cathedral sanctuary in the United States. It is still considered the heart and soul of San Antonio.

Spanish Governor's Palace

A National Historic Landmark, the Spanish Governor's Palace encompasses all that remains of the Presidio San Antonio de Béjar, originally constructed at this location in the early 18th century. The keystone above the main entrance is marked with the coat of arms of Spanish King Ferdinand VI. The adobe and stone structure that once housed officials of the Spanish Province of Texas celebrates San Antonio's earliest history and cultural heritage.

The Menger Hotel

The Menger is the oldest continuously operating hotel west of the Mississippi River. It was built in 1859 by William Menger and has hosted many prominent guests, including thirteen United States presidents. The hotel is known for ghost sightings by hotel guests and employees. The Menger Hotel is registered as a National Historic Hotel.

The Alamo

Originally named Mission San Antonio de Valero, the Alamo was established in 1718 as San Antonio's first mission. The mission was already 100 years old when it fell in the famous Battle of the Alamo and became a battle cry for liberty during the Texas Revolution. The Alamo stands as a memorial to the heroes who sacrificed their lives during the courageous battle.

San Antonio Missions Historical Park

In the 18th century, Missions San Antonio de Valero, Concepción, San Juan, Espada and San José were established along the San Antonio River. The Spanish church used the missions to further its influence into Texas and to convert the native population.

Mission Concepción

Mission Nuestra Señora de la Purisima Concepción de Acuña was moved to San Antonio from East Texas in 1731. Today it stands as the oldest unrestored church in America and looks much like it did in 1731.

Mission San Juan

Mission San Juan Capistrano was originally founded in 1716 in eastern Texas and moved to its current location on the San Antonio River in 1731. The fertile farmland and pastures allowed the Mission to be self-sufficient and it supplied much of the region with produce.

Mission Espada

Mission San Francisco de la Espada was founded in 1660 near Weches, Texas and was the first mission established in Texas. It was moved to it current location in 1731 and has the best-preserved example of the irrigation system that was used to bring water from the river to the fields.

Mission San José

Founded in 1720, Mission San José y San Miguel de Aguayo was the second and largest mission in the area. The mission was restored in the 1930s and serves as an example of how the missions might have looked 250 years ago. La Ventana de Rosa, the Rose Window, located on the south wall of the church sacristy, is considered one of the finest examples of baroque architecture in North America.

Magik Theatre

The Magik Theatre opened in 1994 as an offshoot of the Commerce Street Stage. It is a full-time professional theatre for youth and their families. Magik Theatre strives to develop a child's love and understanding of literature through theatrical performances.

HemisFair Park

HemisFair Park was created to host the 1968 World's Fair that celebrated the confluence of civilizations in the Americas and commemorated the 250th anniversary of San Antonio's founding. The park is home to waterfalls, fountains, a playground, the Institute of Texan Cultures, the Mexican Cultural Institute and the famous Tower of the Americas.

Tower of the Americas

The Tower of the Americas is a 750-foot observation tower with a revolving restaurant. It was built as the signature structure for the 1968 World's Fair.

The Military and San Antonio

In 1719, the Spanish founded San Antonio as a military garrison, beginning a military presence in the area that continues today. San Antonio has been occupied by Conquistadors, Texas Rangers, Union and Confederate troops, and Teddy Roosevelt's Rough Riders. Today San Antonio is home to Joint Base San Antonio, which includes Fort Sam Houston and Brooke Army Medical Center, Lackland Air Force Base and Randolf Air Force Base.

Joint Base San Antonio - Fort Sam Houston

Fort Sam Houston serves as the command headquarters for the United States Army North. The construction of the fort began in the 1870s and today it is one of the Army's oldest installations. The Quadrangle, built in 1876 as a supply depot, is home to the clocktower, which still bears its original inscription and architecture. Sam Houston is home to Brooke Army Medical Center and is known as the "Home of Army Medicine." It is the largest and most important military medical training facility in the United States.

Joint Base San Antonio - Lackland Air Force Base

Lackland Air Force Base is under the jurisdiction of the 802nd Mission Support Group, Air Education and Training Command (AETC). The Base is named after Brigadier General Frank Lackland and has a collection of vintage military aircraft on permanent display on its parade grounds.

Joint Base San Antonio - Randolph Air Force Base

Randolph Air Force Base is under the jurisdiction of the 902nd Mission Support Group, Air Education and Training Command (AETC). The base is home to the 12th Flying Training Wing (12FTW). It is known as "the Showplace of the Air Force" because of the Spanish Colonial Revival Style architecture. Due to its distinctive architecture, the wing's headquarters have become known throughout the Air Force as "the Taj Mahal."

Buckhorn Saloon and Museum

The Buckhorn Saloon & Museum, a privately-run, family-owned museum, was established in 1881 by Albert Friedrich as a saloon. During Prohibition, it was turned into a curio shop and after Prohibition, it was once again a saloon. It was moved twice before being bought by the original Friedrich family in the 1990s and moved to its current location. Today the Buckhorn is known for its unique collection of wildlife trophies and is home to the Texas Ranger Museum.

Paris Hatters

Family-owned and operated since 1917, Paris Hatters is world famous for their expertise in quality fitted and custom-shaped hats. From royalty to ranchers, their clientele enjoys the perfectly suited Stetson. It is the oldest surviving retail business in downtown San Antonio.

San Antonio Stockshow and Rodeo

The San Antonio Stockshow and Rodeo started in 1950 and has grown to be one of the most prestigious events in San Antonio. It is filled with courageous cowboys, exciting concerts, fairgrounds, shopping and educational opportunities.

Mi Tierra

Mi Tierra was opened in 1941 by Pedro and Cruz Cortez and is still family-owned and operated. It is located in Market Square (El Mercado) and is a popular destination for authentic Mexican food.

El Mercado (Market Square)

Market Square is the largest Mexican market in the U.S. with over 100 shops and restaurants. You can always find live music, folkloric dancers, artisans, and mini-fiestas!

La Veladora at the Guadalupe Cultural Arts Center

The Guadalupe was founded in 1980 as a nonprofit, multidisciplinary organization whose mission is to promote and develop the culture and arts of the Chicano/Latino/Native American populations. It does this by focusing on six disciplines: dance, literature, media arts, theater arts, visual arts and music. La Veladora, completed in 2003 by San Antonio artist Jesse Trevino, is a 40-foot mosaic of Our Lady of Guadalupe on the side of the Guadalupe Cultural Arts Center.

San Antonio Symphony

The San Antonio Symphony was founded in 1939 by conductor Max Reiter. The mission of the Symphony is to improve and enrich the community by influencing the artistic fabric of San Antonio through excellent symphonic performance, education and service.

Majestic Theatre

The Majestic is San Antonio's premier performing arts facility. It was designed and built by John Eberson in 1929 for Karl Hoblitzelle's Interstate Theatres. Inspired by Spanish Mission, Baroque, and Mediterranean architectural traditions, theater patrons are transported to a fantasy villa. It is known as one of the most ornate facilities in the country.

Schilo's Delicatessen

Schilo's, an authentic German deli, opened in 1917. It is one of the oldest continually operated restaurants in the State of Texas. Schilo's is known for its homemade root beer, split pea soup and Reuben sandwiches.

Alamodome
The Alamodome is a rectilinear five-level stadium that can accommodate more than 70,000 people. The facility hosts concerts, sports competitions of all sorts, as well as the Alamo Bowl, an annual NCAA football bowl game.

The San Antonio Spurs
Four-time NBA Champions, the Spurs are known as San Antonio's "heroes of the hardwood." They are part of the Southwest Division of the Western Conference in the National Basketball Association.

Museum Reach
Museum Reach stretches north along the San Antonio River and has been enhanced with art installations by local and national artists, waterfalls, landscaping and architecture. Private Funds raised by San Antonio River Improvements Project (SARIP) make this stretch of the river an inspiring and beautiful stroll.

Pearl Brewery
The Pearl, the original site of the Pearl Brewery, is now a culinary and cultural destination in San Antonio. This historic gathering place is where everyone is welcome to eat, play and learn along the banks of the San Antonio River.

San Antonio Museum of Art (SAMA)
The San Antonio Museum of Art opened in 1981 in the historic Lone Star Brewery complex. The Museum anchors the "Museum Reach" expansion of the celebrated San Antonio River Walk. It is known for its American, Asian and Ancient Mediterranean Art. The museum's impressive collection spans five millennia.

Brackenridge Park
Brackenridge Park is made up of 343 acres donated to the city over a period of years beginning in 1899 by Colonel George W. Brackenridge. The park is home to the San Antonio Zoo, the Brackenridge Eagle Miniature Train, the Brackenridge golf course, jogging trails, public art, and an adult and senior center.

Japanese Tea Garden
The Japanese Tea Garden is located adjacent to the Sunken Garden open-air amphitheater in Brackenridge Park. The Garden features an open-air pagoda, beautiful koi ponds, a waterfall and a teahouse.

San Antonio Zoo Eagle
The Brackenridge Eagle Miniature train has been in operation since 1956, when it was the longest miniature train in the world. In 2001, the train was taken over by the zoo and renamed The San Antonio Zoo Eagle. The train is a replica of the original 1863 C.P. Huntington #3 train.

Kiddie Park
Known as "America's oldest children's amusement park," Kiddie Park was established in 1925 and renovated in 2009. The park has many of the original rides, most notably an original 1918 carousel. The park has entertained generations and continues to be a favorite.

San Antonio Zoological Gardens & Aquarium
What is known as the San Antonio Zoo began in 1914 when Colonel George W. Brackenridge placed bison, deer, monkeys, lions and bears on land he deeded to the city. This collection later became the San Antonio Zoo. Today the zoo is home to over 8,500 animals representing 779 different species on 56 acres.

The Witte Museum

Founded in 1926, the Witte Museum boasts historic artifacts, Texas art, textiles, dinosaur bones, prehistoric rock art, wildlife dioramas, the H-E-B Science Treehouse and blockbuster traveling exhibits. Experience the legendary history of South Texas in the South Texas Heritage Center featuring Davy Crockett's fiddle, Sam Houston's sash, a Colt Walker revolver, live gallery theater in a river-front amphitheater and more.

San Antonio Botanical Garden

The Botanical Garden, which opened in 1980, is a 38-acre living museum. The gardens include floral displays, a native forest walk, glass conservatories and historic log cabins.

McNay Art Museum

Built by artist and educator Marion Koogler McNay in the 1920s, the Spanish Colonial Revival residence opened as Texas' first museum of modern art in 1954. The museum, which sits on 23 landscaped acres, is home to one of the finest collections of contemporary art and sculpture in the Southwestern United States.

San Antonio Central Library

The Central Library opened in 1995 in downtown San Antonio. The building is painted "enchilada red" and is a Mexican Modernist design by renowned Mexican architect Ricardo Legorreta.

King William Historic District

The King William Historic District was established by prominent German merchants during the 1840s and is known for its beautiful historic homes. The area was restored in the 1960s and became a Nationally Registered Historic District in 1972.

Carl H. Guenther House

This elegant home was built in 1859 by Carl Hilmar Guenther, the founder of Pioneer Flour Mills. Pioneer is the oldest continuously operating flour mill in the United States. The home, now a museum, also has a gift shop, banquet facilities and a restaurant known for its delicious freshly baked biscuits, fluffy pancakes and pastries.

Fiesta® San Antonio!

Fiesta®, an annual festival held every April, started in 1891 as a one-parade event organized to honor the heroes from the battles of the Alamo and San Jacinto. Today, Fiesta has grown into an eleven day celebration of San Antonio's rich heritage. Coronations of local "royalty," parades and a carnival are only a few of the more than 100 events run by nonprofits that take place throughout the city.

SeaWorld® San Antonio

SeaWorld® San Antonio, the world's largest marine life park, offers an exciting and educational blend of marine-life shows, rides and attractions. For up-close animal encounters, the park offers a variety of programs with beluga whales, sea lions, penguins and more. An added attraction is Aquatica®, a whimsical waterpark with up-close animal experiences, high-speed thrills, and relaxing, sandy beaches.

Natural Bridge Caverns

Natural Bridge Caverns, located 30 minutes north of downtown San Antonio, were discovered by four students from Saint Mary's University in the 1960s. Now a popular destination for explorers and tourists alike, the still active and growing caverns are family-owned and operated. They are part of the largest known caverns in the state of Texas and never cease to amaze with their natural beauty.